A Band of Brave Men
The Story of the 54th Massachusetts Regiment

by Ellen Dreyer

CELEBRATION PRESS
Pearson Learning Group

The following people from **Pearson Learning Group** have contributed to the development of this product:

Leslie Feierstone Barna, Cindy Kane **Editorial**
Stephen Barth, Joan Mazzeo **Design**
Salita Mehta **Photo Research**
Dan Trush **Art Buying**

Marketing Christine Fleming
Publishing Operations Jennifer Van Der Heide
Production/Manufacturing Laura Benford-Sullivan, Susan Levine, Michele Uhl

Content Area Consultant Dr. Daniel J. Gelo

The following people from **DK** have contributed to the development of this program:

Art Director Rachael Foster
Scarlett O'Hara **Managing Editor** | **Editor UK Editions** Marie Greenwood

Photo Credits: All photographs are by David Mager, Elbaliz Mendez, and Judy Mahoney of the Pearson Learning Group Photo Studio except as noted below.
All photography © Pearson Education, Inc. (PEI) unless otherwise specifically noted.

Front Cover: *t.* North Wind Picture Archives/Nancy Carter; *m.l.* DK Images; *b.l.* DK Images/Gettysburg National Military Park. Back Cover: © Tria Giovan/Corbis. 1: Linda Whitwam/DK Images. 3: © Scala/Art Resource, NY. 5: *t.* Glenbow Museum; *b.* The Granger Collection. 6: David Wagner/The Rhode Island Black Heritage Society. 7: *t.* The Granger Collection; *b.* Dave King/DK Images. 8: *t.* Courtesy of the Massachusetts Historical Society, Boston; *b.* © Bettmann/Corbis. 9: *t.* Massachusetts Commandery Military Order of the Loyal Legion and the US Army Military History Institute; *b.* Courtesy of the Massachusetts Historical Society, Boston. 10: Florida State Archives. 11: Courtesy of the Massachusetts Historical Society, Boston. 12: Edwin L. Jackson. 13: *l.* Courtesy of the Massachusetts Historical Society, Boston; *r.* © Corbis. 14: © Corbis. 14–15: © Tria Giovan/Corbis. 15–19: © Corbis. 20: *t.* © Corbis; *b.* © Tria Giovan/Corbis. 21: Private Collection/Bridgeman Art Library. 22: Courtesy, Library of Congress. 23: *t.* Congressional Medal of Honor Society; *b.* Michael Gratnek, Jr. 24: *t.* © Bettmann/Corbis; *b.* National Archives, Records of the Adjutant General's Office, 1780's–1917. 25: © Corbis. 26: *t.* © Medford Historical Society Collection/Corbis; *b.* © Tria Giovan/Corbis. 27: Florida State Archives. 28: William S. Nawrocki/Nawrocki Stock Photo, Inc. 29: Florida State Archives. 30: Courtesy of the Massachusetts Historical Society, Boston.
Illustration: 4, 16: XNR Productions.

For information regarding licensing and permissions, write to Rights and Permissions Department, Pearson Learning Group, 299 Jefferson Road, Parsippany, NJ 07054 USA or to Rights and Permissions Department, DK Publishing, The Penguin Group (UK), 80 Strand, London WC2R 0RL

Lexile is a U.S. registered trademark of MetaMetrics, Inc. All right reserved.

ISBN: 0-7652-5247-3

Color reproduction by Colourscan, Singapore
Printed in the United States of America
7 8 9 10   08 07 06

1-800-321-3106
www.pearsonlearning.com

Contents

A Golden Opportunity

In 1861, a war began in the United States when fighting broke out between the northern and southern states. This conflict came to be known as the Civil War. Why did the states fight? By 1861, the southern states, called the **Confederacy**, had **seceded**, or separated, from the rest of the country. They wished to form their own nation apart from the United States. They wanted to have their own government.

The northern states were known as the **Union**. Unlike the southern states, they wanted to keep the United States as one nation.

By June 1861, eleven southern states had seceded from the Union. West Virginia did not secede and became a state in 1863.

The South and the North were different in many ways in 1861. Most people in the South made their living from farming. Large southern farms, called plantations, grew cotton, tobacco, and other crops. Plantation owners depended on slave labor. Vast numbers of enslaved African Americans worked in

the fields and as house servants. The southern slave owners did not want to end a practice that made them wealthy.

In contrast, many people in the North worked in industries. Factory workers might work very long hours for low pay, but, unlike slaves, they were paid for their work.

Labor in the South (above), where plantation owners depended on enslaved African Americans, was very different from that in the North (below), which had many factories.

All African Americans, whether free or enslaved, wanted better lives in a more just society. Many were willing to risk their life for these goals. One **freeman** in New Orleans told a Union general that he would fight as long as he could, "if only my boy may stand in the street equal to a white boy when the war is over."

African Americans had fought and died in the Revolutionary War and the War of 1812. Yet when the Civil War began, African Americans weren't allowed to join the U.S. Army. They could only serve in positions such as cook or musician. Many white people had the **prejudiced** view that African Americans could not be good soldiers.

Mural by David Wagner courtesy of
The Rhode Island Black Heritage Society

African Americans such as the soldiers shown in this painting fought in the Revolutionary War.

The Abolitionist Movement

By 1850, it was illegal to own slaves in most northern states. In part, this was thanks to the efforts of **abolitionists**—people, both black and white, who wanted to end slavery. One of the most famous was Harriet Tubman. Before the war, Tubman was a "conductor" for the Underground Railroad, helping more than 300 enslaved African Americans escape to freedom. During the war, she served as a soldier, a spy, and a nurse.

Harriet Tubman

Then, in January 1863, President Abraham Lincoln issued the Emancipation Proclamation. This document said that because the South would not rejoin the Union, the slaves would be freed. As a result, 3 million enslaved African Americans gained their freedom. Abolitionists celebrated with speeches and songs.

By the end of January, Lincoln had given permission for African American men to **enlist** in the Union army and navy. Large numbers of men volunteered. They were very much needed, for the war had been going on for nearly two years. There was no sign that it would end.

a cap worn by a Union infantryman, or foot soldier

7

Courtesy of the Massachusetts Historical Society, Boston

Robert Gould Shaw

Born on October 10, 1837, Robert Gould Shaw grew up in a wealthy family. His parents were both abolitionists. In 1860, Shaw enlisted in the army. One year later he received an officer's commission. Shaw fought in several battles. He was wounded in the bloody Battle of Antietam, Maryland, on September 17, 1862.

Colonel Robert Gould Shaw

In February 1863, Governor John A. Andrew of Massachusetts began **recruiting** for a new **regiment** of African American soldiers: the Fifty-fourth Massachusetts Regiment. It was one of the first African American fighting regiments to be formed. Andrew asked an abolitionist, twenty-five-year-old Captain Robert Gould Shaw, to lead the Fifty-fourth, and promoted Shaw to the rank of colonel.

Recruitment offices were set up in several northern cities. Leading abolitionists such as Frederick Douglass, a former slave, gave speeches urging men to enlist in the Fifty-fourth. Many did.

Frederick Douglass

Lieutenant Colonel Edward N. Hallowell became second-in-command of the Fifty-fourth. Training began for the new soldiers. They were based at Camp Meigs, just outside Boston.

Lieutenant Colonel Edward N. Hallowell

Some African American soldiers in the Fifty-fourth proved their leadership and became officers. However, the government would not allow African Americans to be **commissioned**. They could not become higher-ranked officers, those who hold the rank of lieutenant or higher. One of the African American officers was Sergeant Major Lewis H. Douglass. He was one of two sons of Frederick Douglass to serve in the Fifty-fourth.

a recruiting poster for the Fifty-fourth Regiment

TO COLORED MEN.
54th
REGIMENT!
MASSACHUSETTS VOLUNTEERS,
OF
☞ AFRICAN DESCENT!
$100 BOUNTY!
At the expiration of the term of service.
PAY, $13 A MONTH!
AND
STATE AID TO FAMILIES.
RECRUITING OFFICE,
Cor. Cambridge & North Russell Sts., Boston.
Lieut. J. W. M. APPLETON, Recruiting Officer.
J. E. FARWELL & Co., Steam Job Printers, No. 37 Congress Street, Boston.

Jeremiah Rolls,
first sergeant

John H. Wilson,
sergeant major

Abram C. Simms,
corporal

Who were the men of the Fifty-fourth Regiment? Over the course of the Civil War, approximately 1,700 men enlisted in the regiment. They came not only from Massachusetts, but also from Pennsylvania, New York, and Ohio, all of which had large African American populations. Some came from as far away as Canada and the West Indies. At least thirty of the men had been enslaved.

The men were mainly in their early twenties, and most had worked as laborers and farmers. Others had been barbers, waiters, cooks, stonecutters, sailors, glassmakers, and cabinetmakers, among other professions.

Isom Ampey,
private

George Lipscomb, corporal, and
Thomas Bowman, sergeant

From Disappointment to Victory

Spirits were high in late May 1863 when the men of the Fifty-fourth were given their first assignment. They sailed by steamship to Hilton Head, South Carolina, arriving in early June.

Shaw and his men had counted on going into battle quickly, but they did not fight right away. Instead, the regiment was moved to St. Simon's Island, Georgia. There, Shaw reported to Colonel James Montgomery, head of the Second South Carolina Regiment. It, too, was an African American regiment.

Montgomery took the two regiments to Darien, Georgia. When they arrived, the small town was nearly deserted. Montgomery ordered the men to raid, loot, and then burn the town.

Charles H. Arnum, private

John Goosberry, private

Shaw was angry about Montgomery's decision to destroy Darien. In a letter to his wife, Annie, he wrote that Montgomery had told him that "the Southerners must be made to feel that this was a real war." Shaw added, "I myself don't like it." So far, he felt that he had acted with honor in the war, but the Darien raid was shameful in his eyes.

Shaw was also worried about how the Darien raid would reflect on his soldiers. In his letter to Annie, he wrote: "I am not sure that it will not harm very much the reputation of black troops and those connected with them." He was worried that his men's reputation would indeed be harmed.

The raid on Darien, Georgia, is remembered in this marker in present-day Darien.

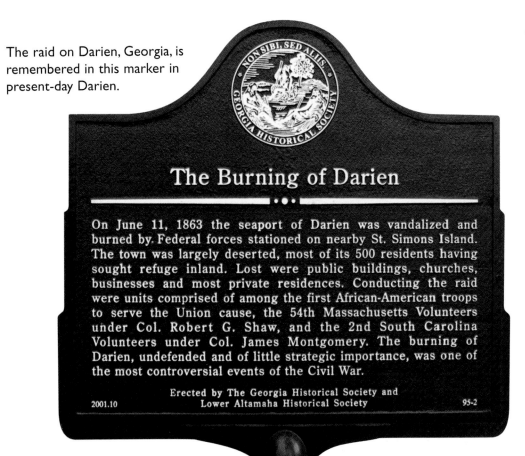

NON SIBI, SED ALIIS.
GEORGIA HISTORICAL SOCIETY

The Burning of Darien

On June 11, 1863 the seaport of Darien was vandalized and burned by Federal forces stationed on nearby St. Simons Island. The town was largely deserted, most of its 500 residents having sought refuge inland. Lost were public buildings, churches, businesses and most private residences. Conducting the raid were units comprised of among the first African-American troops to serve the Union cause, the 54th Massachusetts Volunteers under Col. Robert G. Shaw, and the 2nd South Carolina Volunteers under Col. James Montgomery. The burning of Darien, undefended and of little strategic importance, was one of the most controversial events of the Civil War.

Erected by The Georgia Historical Society and Lower Altamaha Historical Society

2001.10   95-2

Sergeant Henry Steward of the Fifty-fourth Massachusetts, left, and the Massachusetts soldier shown at right, a white man, received unequal pay.

Shaw had another struggle on his hands. The government had promised equal pay to African American troops. The soldiers expected to make the same amount, thirteen dollars a month, that other soldiers received. Instead, they were paid only ten dollars a month. The African American soldiers also had to pay three dollars a month for their uniforms, so the monthly pay was really only seven dollars.

Shaw decided to protest by refusing any payment for his officers and his soldiers. He hoped this would make the government change its mind.

In this Civil War photo, torpedoes and other ammunition sit in the yard of Charleston's **arsenal**.

The regiment had returned to South Carolina after the Darien raid. The men now prepared for their first battle. They would be part of a Union effort to capture the city of Charleston, South Carolina.

Charleston was important to the Confederacy. It was a wealthy port city at the meeting place of two rivers, and goods were shipped in and out of its harbor. From Charleston, Confederate soldiers and military supplies were taken inland.

Capturing Charleston was a major goal for the North. It would strike a strong blow to the Confederacy.

The Fifty-fourth landed on James Island, South Carolina. On July 16, 1863, they came under fire for the first time.

Three companies of the Fifty-fourth were on **picket** duty near the southern tip of the island. At dawn on July 16, the soldiers heard gunshots ring out. Shaw organized his men just in time before hundreds of Confederate soldiers charged them.

The Confederates were angry when they saw the men of the Fifty-fourth Regiment before them. Here were African American soldiers, fighting them on equal ground.

This photo from another Civil War battle shows African American soldiers on picket duty.

a rifle from the Civil War

The Confederates' goal was to capture the Tenth Connecticut Regiment. The Fifty-fourth ran toward the enemy, firing back at them. This gave the Tenth Connecticut time to retreat. The Fifty-fourth continued to fight fiercely, using hand-to-hand combat at times.

When the battle ended, the Fifty-fourth had lost fourteen men. Eighteen more were wounded, and thirteen were taken prisoner. The Connecticut troops visited the Massachusetts camp to thank the men of the Fifty-fourth. Their bravery was also praised by the general in charge of the battle.

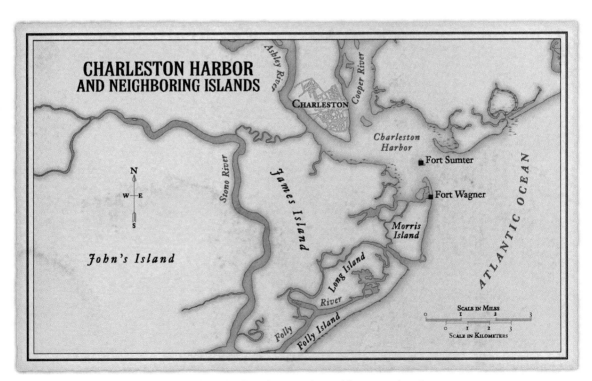

This map shows Charleston, South Carolina, and neighboring islands.

The troops boarded a steamship like this one to cross the Folly River. The Union would often capture Confederate steamships and rename them for Union use.

News spread quickly of the Fifty-fourth's courage on James Island. Just as Shaw had hoped, this victory brought respect to his regiment. The event also helped to ease his shame over the Darien raid.

The weary troops of the Fifty-fourth had no time to eat or rest. Late in the evening of July 16, they received orders to march.

The soldiers tramped all night through a raging thunderstorm. They had to cross narrow bridges to move from island to island. A steamship took them across the Folly River. Finally, they reached their destination: Morris Island, the location of a heavily armed Confederate fort called Fort Wagner.

> ### "A Fortunate Day"
> Shaw wrote to his wife Annie about the James Island battle: "You don't know what a fortunate day this has been for me and for us all, excepting some poor fellows who were killed and wounded. . . . General Terry sent me word he was highly gratified with the behavior of my men, and the officers and privates of other regiments praise us very much."

A Band of Brave Men

Fort Wagner spanned the northern tip of Morris Island. To take control of this island, the Union army would first have to capture the fort.

Although the structure was made of sand and logs, it was very solid. The walls were 30 feet tall, and the ceiling was topped with 10 feet of sand.

However, the Union commanders, General Quincy A. Gillmore and General Truman Seymour, still thought they could destroy the fort. They ordered a massive shelling attack on the fort from land and sea. The generals believed that cannon fire would weaken the structure so it could be taken by a ground attack. They also thought only a few hundred Confederate soldiers were inside.

Federal soldiers erected structures called batteries to put cannons in place for the attack on Fort Wagner.

Cannons like these were used to bombard Fort Wagner.

In both cases, the generals were wrong. The fort's thick walls held up against the cannon fire. Instead of several hundred, 1,700 Confederate soldiers waited inside!

Early in the evening of July 18, Shaw learned that the Fifty-fourth was to fight in the front lines at Fort Wagner. The commander in charge of the attack was Brigadier General George C. Strong. He told Shaw, "You may lead the column, if you say 'yes.' Your men, I know, are worn out, but do as you choose." Shaw immediately accepted.

A Well-Defended Fort

In its day, Fort Wagner was considered a marvel. Its double southern walls were built of sand, turf, and palmetto logs. The fort was protected by seventeen artillery guns. To the east was a marsh that could not be crossed. Beyond lay the Atlantic Ocean. At high tide, a narrow strip of ground led up to the fort. This made a ground attack difficult.

Fort Wagner

No food rations had arrived on Morris Island, and there was no time to sleep. The tired, hungry men got ready for battle.

The plan was for the Fifty-fourth to approach the fort on foot. When the soldiers were within 100 yards of the fort, they would charge and attack with **bayonets**. Afterward, several other regiments would join the fight.

Shaw walked among his men as night began to fall. He told them that he wanted them to prove themselves in this battle. Then he took his position at the head of the regiment.

Hardtack, a hard biscuit, was typical food served to troops on the move.

The Fifty-fourth set out, marching quickly over three-quarters of a mile. The guns of Wagner remained silent, but guns from Fort Sumter and other nearby forts fired on the men.

Because the beach was so narrow, some of the men marched through ocean water. When the men were about 200 yards from the fort, the Confederates opened fire. Sergeant Lewis Douglass would write about the experience: "Not a man flinched, although it was a trying time. A shell would explode and clear a space of 20 feet; our men would close up again."

the nighttime attack on Fort Wagner, as drawn by an illustrator

This dramatic illustration shows the Fifty-fourth Regiment's attack on Fort Wagner.

It was a gruesome scene. Hundreds of troops were killed instantly. As Captain Luis F. Emilio later wrote: "Wagner became a mound of fire, from which poured a stream of shot and shell. . . . A sheet of flame, followed by a running fire, like electric sparks, swept along the **parapet**." Yet the Fifty-fourth continued its advance, breaking into a run toward the walls of the fort.

Shaw led his men up to the parapet. "Forward, Fifty-fourth!" he shouted. Then a gunshot pierced his chest. He fell backwards, dead. His body would be buried the next day, along with many of his men.

Colonel Hallowell, Shaw's second-in-command, had been wounded. A small number of men from the Fifty-fourth reached one corner of the fort. They struggled with the Confederates, but the outnumbered Union soldiers were forced to fall back.

The men showed great bravery throughout the battle. Sergeant William H. Carney saw the soldier who was carrying the regiment's flag fall in battle. He took the flag and carried it into the fort, where he was badly wounded. "I have only done my duty," he said after retreating safely with the flag. "The old flag never touched the ground." For his actions, Carney was later awarded the Medal of Honor.

the Medal of Honor

Sergeant William H. Carney won a Medal of Honor for his bravery in battle.

Many Union soldiers were killed or wounded in the battle.

The battle cost the Union side dearly: 1,515 soldiers were dead, wounded, or missing, including 111 officers. By contrast, the entire Confederate side had only 181 **casualties**. Among the Union casualties were 281 of the 600 men from the Fifty-fourth who went into battle.

Despite such heavy losses, there was a positive side to the battle. It brought a deeper respect for all African American troops. As Frederick Douglass observed, the terrible battle had done more to end objections about the quality of African Americans as soldiers than "a century of ordinary life and observation" might have achieved.

a list of the Fifty-fourth's men missing after the Battle of Fort Wagner

"Three Cheers for Massachusetts!"

The Battle of Fort Wagner brought fame to the Fifty-fourth. Many new recruits joined the Union army. These included freemen from the North as well as recently freed African American slaves from southern states.

The Union army and navy continued their attack on Fort Wagner. They used a new strategy: a **siege**. This time, the men of the Fifty-fourth and other Union troops fought with shovels. They dug trenches, where guns were placed to bombard Fort Wagner and other forts around Charleston. The Union did not spare the city itself. To the terror of Charleston's citizens, the same long-range guns firing on the forts were turned on the city.

Finally, on September 6, the Confederates abandoned Fort Wagner. They also gave up another fort at the northeastern tip of Morris Island.

the bombing of forts in Charleston Harbor by the Union military

General Quincy A. Gillmore

Early in 1864, under orders from General Gillmore, the Fifty-fourth went to Florida. The regiment's new leader was Colonel Edward N. Hallowell.

There were several reasons for the Florida campaign. President Lincoln was eager to make Florida part of the Union once again. Also, Florida produced cotton, lumber, beef, and other supplies that would be useful to the Union army. Finally, General Gillmore wanted to find recruits in Florida for new African American regiments.

The Fifty-fourth was part of a large Union force that occupied Jacksonville, Florida. It was soon given the order to march.

Civil War drums used by regiments in several states, including Massachusetts

the fighting at Olustee

Confederate troops were gathering in northeast Florida, near a stop on a railroad line called Olustee Station, to fight the Union invaders. The Fifty-fourth arrived at Olustee Station on February 20. Soldiers of the Fifty-fourth joined many other Union soldiers, including several African American regiments organized under the Bureau of Colored Troops.

The Confederates were waiting in trenches and behind earthworks. Each side had approximately 5,000 soldiers, but the Confederates were much better prepared. After four hours of intense fighting, the Union side had about 1,800 casualties. The Confederate casualties were only half that many. The Union had lost the battle.

The U.S. Colored Troops

Massachusetts was one of the first states to raise African American regiments. These regiments were not thought to be part of the U.S. Bureau of Colored Troops, which was created in May 1863 to recruit African American soldiers. That is why the letters USCT, used to identify those regiments formed by the Bureau, are not part of the Fifty-fourth's name.

After their defeat at Olustee, the Union forces retreated to Jacksonville. In April, the Fifty-fourth was ordered back to South Carolina, where the soldiers guarded a prison camp on Morris Island.

Meanwhile, steps were being taken in the government to make the African American soldiers' pay equal to that of white soldiers. The inequality of pay was still a bitter subject for African American troops. This feeling was reflected in the battle cry of the Fifty-fourth Regiment: "Three cheers for Massachusetts and seven dollars a month!"

Finally, in June 1864, a law passed that settled the matter. African American soldiers were granted full and equal pay, with credit for back pay due to them.

African American soldiers were finally granted equal pay in June 1864.

Mustering Out

Another important victory for all African American troops came in 1864. Sergeant Stephen A. Swails of the Fifty-fourth received an officer's commission. Governor Andrew of Massachusetts promoted him to the rank of lieutenant.

After this, other deserving African American soldiers became officers. However, it was only the beginning of the fight for equality in the military. Many white officers were angry that the government had decided that African Americans could serve as officers. They thought these commissions should go to white soldiers. Still, Governor Andrew's action was an important advance.

After the war, Stephen Swails became a lawyer and a state senator—in South Carolina, where the Fifty-fourth had fought so bravely.

The Fifty-fourth fought in several more battles. One was at Honey Hill, South Carolina, in November 1864. Another took place at Boykin's Mill, South Carolina, in April 1865. That same month, the Confederates surrendered. The war was over.

Veterans of the Fifty-fourth gathered in Boston in 1897 at the dedication of a memorial to Shaw and the regiment.

In August 1865, the regiment was discharged, or "mustered out." On September 2, people lined the streets of Boston to cheer the returning regiment.

The men of the Fifty-fourth Massachusetts Regiment are still remembered today. A memorial to Robert Gould Shaw and the regiment was dedicated in Boston, Massachusetts, in 1897. In 1989, the film *Glory* was released. The film's popularity brought new attention to the story of the brave soldiers of the Fifty-fourth Massachusetts.

A Timeline of the Fifty-fourth Massachusetts Regiment

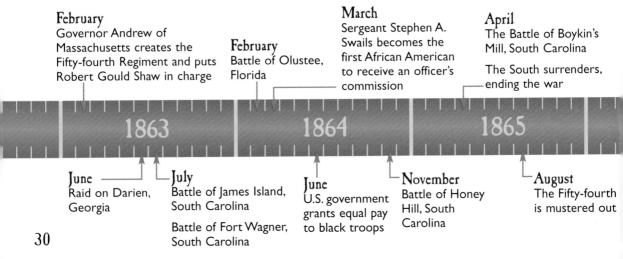

February
Governor Andrew of Massachusetts creates the Fifty-fourth Regiment and puts Robert Gould Shaw in charge

February
Battle of Olustee, Florida

March
Sergeant Stephen A. Swails becomes the first African American to receive an officer's commission

April
The Battle of Boykin's Mill, South Carolina

The South surrenders, ending the war

1863

1864

1865

June
Raid on Darien, Georgia

July
Battle of James Island, South Carolina

Battle of Fort Wagner, South Carolina

June
U.S. government grants equal pay to black troops

November
Battle of Honey Hill, South Carolina

August
The Fifty-fourth is mustered out

Glossary

abolitionists   people who were opposed to slavery

arsenal   a place where weapons are stored

bayonets   steel blades at the end of rifles

casualties   military persons lost through death, injuries, or capture, or through being missing in action

commissioned   recognized as an officer by the government

Confederacy   the southern states that seceded from the United States

enlist   to join the armed forces

freeman   an African American who was born free or became free

parapet   a wall of earth or stone to protect soldiers

picket   a soldier who guards an army from a surprise attack

prejudiced   holding a dislike or distrust of people because of their race, religion, or country

recruiting   finding new soldiers for the armed forces

regiment   a military unit

seceded   separated

siege   a military action blocking people and supplies from reaching a strategic location

Union   the union of northern states during the Civil War

Index